Breath and Bone

FINAL EXHALE

Joannes Bernardinus, 17th century

BREATH AND BONE

BY

KELLY LYNN CURRY

WESTMINSTER

ARCHIBALD CONSTABLE AND COMPANY

2 WHITEHALL GARDENS

1897

*To the one who inspires me to feel the vastness
of every moment of every day.*

I WRITE TO REMEMBER EVERY FEEL-ING, EVERY BREATH, TO RECREATE MOMENTS: TRAGIC AND BEAUTIFUL, SO I CAN REMEMBER HOW DEEP AND BOUNDLESS THE SPAN OF HUMAN EMOTION REALLY IS.

I'M LOST IN MY HEAD

WHILE CURLED IN MY BED

AN ACHE SO PROFOUND

YEARNING TO MEAN MORE

THAN JUST BREATH AND BONE.

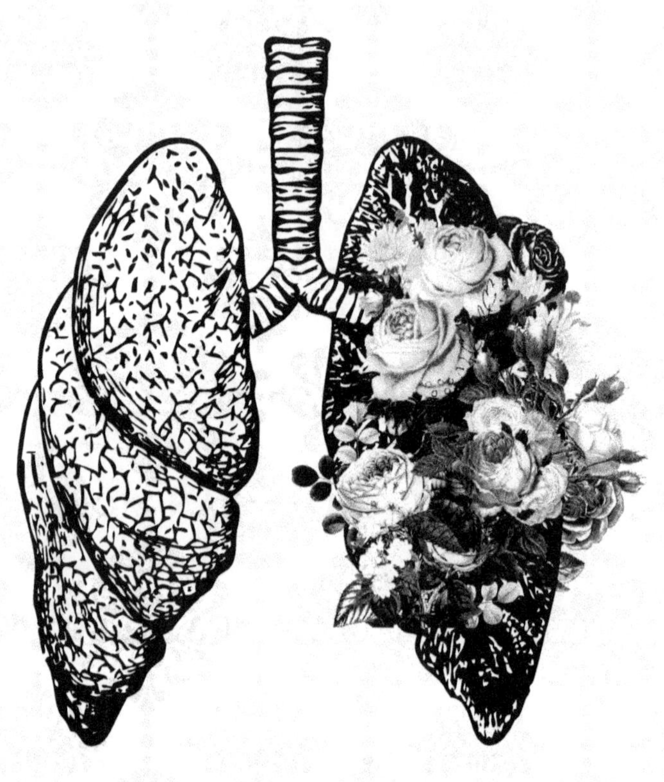

Breath

Puppet Master

Oh what a delicate
Balance we breathe
When we balance our
Head and heart from strings

BLUSH AND BLONDE

Do you ever lay there, and life just bleeds into shades of black and gray? Nothing more than unacceptable nothingness, worthless parts? I've been there, but I close my eyes and remember the first kiss, the first touch, the first smile, and life begins to bleed back in and you can't remember how it could be void of blush and blonde and fiery red or the grey-blue eyes.

GOOSEBUMPS

It feels like I'm breathing in nostalgia,
Certain memories resonate on my skin.

Untitled

There's a junkyard dog
 in the pit of my stomach
Tugging on its chain
It is never truly tamed
Never completely sated
Rough, one ear torn from battles fought
It spends its days pacing
Its nights howling at the moon
Waiting. Always waiting.

EVERLASTING

As I write
The ink bleeds
My thoughts into the fibers
Forever intertwined
This moment everlasting
Even in its quietness
It seems so loud in my ears

Emotional Vampire

It's a suffocating feeling, overwhelming, self-loathing. I ache with the knowledge you are out there, holding a fragment of my heart unknowingly, dragging it through the wreckage of what was once so beautiful.

Every blink is a flash, a memory. Nostalgia. A 9mm to the chest. Sometimes it's overwhelming, all-consuming, and humanity itself is unbearable.

So, I hide. Away from everything, but the memories. I count the hours, the minutes, the seconds until the anguish, this paralyzing heartbreak subsides, and these tears dry but it seems the second that they do a swift motion of fresh pain comes and reminds me of crippling nothingness I'm left with.

Love doesn't seem worth it on this side of the road. I've lost him, he dies and, in his place, resides a demon who bares his face.

He always did call himself an *emotional vampire*.

A Haunting

You are a ghost
You haunt my dreams,
My very existence

WILD AT HEART

When meek and fragile are the fur I shed
and Wild is the only one I know how to wear anymore

Broken Bones

Frustration seeping through my bones
Cracking the calcium at the core
Knocking me to my knees
My skeleton splinters

Walking Dead

To mourn the loss of someone still breathing
An ache so deep it makes the ocean resemble a drop in a puddle
A weakness that pulls you deep into the darkness of your soul,
Reminding you that their breath once held your presence
A void instilled, stitched with memories bloodied with our past
Yet somehow, I cannot shake the taste of caring

Colorblind

I am haunted by the memories
everything used to be so VIBRANT
now it's shades of black and gray

Pyromaniac

A dull ember, a trickle of flame that builds,
 even it should be snuffed out;

you appreciate the warmth it brings even if unreliable
and dangerous.

A fire that will consume, maim, fully engulf your
entire essence, unless it is constantly watched from a
safe distance.

 No, it's better just to be dowsed before anything can
harm because even the smallest of flames can scar.

Cannon Fodder

Our hearts are cannon fodder
Brought a gun to a knife fight
Thumping to the sound of the firing squad
It's like a 45 straight to the heart

INK

I want to be free of his presence
that's been tattooed on my skin
his memories burned on my body

You saw nothing but a breathing carcass,
I saw a beautiful mosaic of every battle he'd won.

Bodyguard

When I'm with you
My demons run
They fear your voice,
your warm embrace.

To Catch A Thief

Fighting my instincts to
Reach out
To beg, borrow, steal back
My heart

ENOLA GAY

I opened up to you
it ended like Hiroshima
My heart: an atomic bomb site

Macabre

There's a hollowness inside my rib cage
Where the bats slumber
The chaos is laid to rest
If only temporarily
At night they rage inside me
Reminding me I'm alive
and something to be reckoned with

Hurricane

A storm raging inside me
Ill effects
        I wish this metaphorical sea
        would calm so
        I could have some peace.

Opened old wounds last night. The proverbial can of worms. It didn't end well, and I don't know why I expected differently.

Untitled

The ache has dulled
The howling quieted
My mourning come and passed
Memories burned thoroughly

Fleeting Moments

Those fleeting moments, somehow epic.
Even if only lasting an instant.
Our first kiss; it was so picturesque.
The fog, the scent of the passing rain still lingering,
my spine-tingling.
I couldn't help but smile.
That moment forever burned in my soul.

Skin Signs

I stripped down to the bare universe inside me
To nothing more than constellations and conversations

Time Bomb

You are living in my veins
like a disease
lying dormant

TORN APART

You tore the soft spot for you from my chest
and laid it to rest
I cannot breathe when I am not whole
For I am a restless soul

Viper

Like a toxic venom
Your love slithers under my skin
In my veins; it burns
I yearn,

The Night

The night consumes
It is like a fog
That seeps into the bones
Happiness purged
engulfed into the oblivion of torment

WONDERLAND

I'm falling down the rabbit hole again
Dangerous and unforgiving
Disastrous consequences
But I can't help but close my eyes and take the plunge
Because the siren's song is so so sweet

Untitled

My heart is hurting
My body aches
I'm lost without your warm embrace

Solitary Confinement

I feel so alone.
       Utterly, positively, alone.

It's night when I feel like I'm going to fall apart.
I'm crumbling.
His words, his actions
       He left me here in this darkness to fend for myself

       I'm just so tired.
          Tired of being alone
             Let down
             Keeping these walls up
             Never being loved
             Never having an intact heart

I want those warm hands wrapped around me while I sleep
Murmuring
The calmness, the sense of safety

I Love You,

I love you.
I'll shout it from the rooftops,
I'll sing it from the shorelines,
I'll whisper it from the pillow next to yours.

TELESCOPE

Constellations
          In your eyes
A glitter, a shimmer, a glow

Untitled

The darkness is back,
and it's cracked my ribs.
Breaking them into a million pieces,
impossible to put back together
but so easy to watch them fall apart.
The hole is gapping.

Genie

I am lying in bed wishing grand wishes that float around the
                    room swirling
          in and out
of my ears as the music dances
                    to the tap of my toes
and my eyelashes flutter
                    like moths to the flame
of the dying candle
                    on the side of my bed
                    and I feel the quietness pull me closer still.

IN THE QUIET

In the silence,
In the stillness,
My heart beats for you.

CADAVER

Staring at the ceiling,
I want to be devoid of all feeling.
I'm plagued with these unwanted thoughts,
As every inch of me slowly rots

RESURRECTION

It has always been about the simple things.
The one thing that drives you to go on.
Almost dying twice,
You remember exactly those moments
that brought you back,
When you stop breathing
stop fighting and it's burning
when you start to cave and accept it:
There's a flash
a tiny spark at the end of your consciousness.
It drives you to fight,
to bring you back,
to everything you ever lived for.

Not Just a Monster Under My Bed

I felt like a dog-eared page he came back to every night. Something worn down, withered; my spirit was broken like the spine of an old library book.

Four in the morning and I couldn't sleep. I was reliving every second from the night before. From the past month of nights. Haunting me, trying to rip my sanity from me.

I was unable to sleep with these memories flowing through me, humming inside. Still shaking, nothing seemed to calm my nerves; they had been stretched to the point of almost snapping.

I thought I could sleep but when my eyes closed my mind conjured a dark figure unknown and replayed every minuscule detail. I knew he would come at four a.m.

There was no fight or flight. I was completely frozen, eyes shut, trying to make it to the next moment. It was sheer horror. Panic. Crushing fear.

When breathing became a monumental task, labored and shadowed, concentrating on it was overwhelming. I could feel my heartbeat through my chest, throbbing in my ears, my blood flowing with absolute terror.

My entire body ached with tense paralyzed muscles, clutching the pillow, and counting the seconds. I tried to move a single inch, just one, in hopes of breaking free but every attempt seemed impossible. If only I could move, I could call for help.

A tyrant was assaulting my door, trying to force the hinges with sheer force. Silence and noise clashed with each other as every punishing vibration echoed through my apartment.

I felt like a child hiding under their covers waiting for the monster to go back under the bed, except my monster was real and charging my door.

My large Siamese cat brushed his tail against my flushed cheeks and howled as he tried to wake me from my state. He pawed, nipped, and scratched as he alerted me to the danger. I could hear the hinges of my front door slowly giving way as he threw himself at it one more time.

A dark figure was suddenly above me, his movements hasty like a demon coming out of the shadows. Sweat and cigarette smoke invaded my nostrils as he stalked towards me.

He slid on top of me and his hands slithered to my neck in a vice grip. My primal needs to flee finally kicked in and I squirmed under the weight of him. He pressed his mouth against mine, the stubble of his chin scrapping against my cheeks, irritating my entire body.

I raked my nails deep into his arms, feeling the skin embed underneath them. I tried to draw blood, to make him feel every ounce of pain he had been inflicting on me for the past 31 nights.

He recoiled, swearing, and swung his fist, landing on my left temple. He yanked the covers away that had been protecting my body from his assault. I tried to knee him, but the bedding only entangled me more.

The sheer weight of his body was making it impossible to fight back. Every moment of lectures on self-protection was running through my head but nothing seemed to be working.

I went for his face when he started pawing at my shirt. I dug deep into his cheeks, letting the blood trickle down onto me. He slapped me before landing his fists on my face a few more times.

It didn't hurt; I had become numb with an overload of pain assaulting every neuron in my body. Adrenaline had overtaken my system.

I tried to scream but my throat was bruised. The sounds resembled a strangled animal. I felt like one.

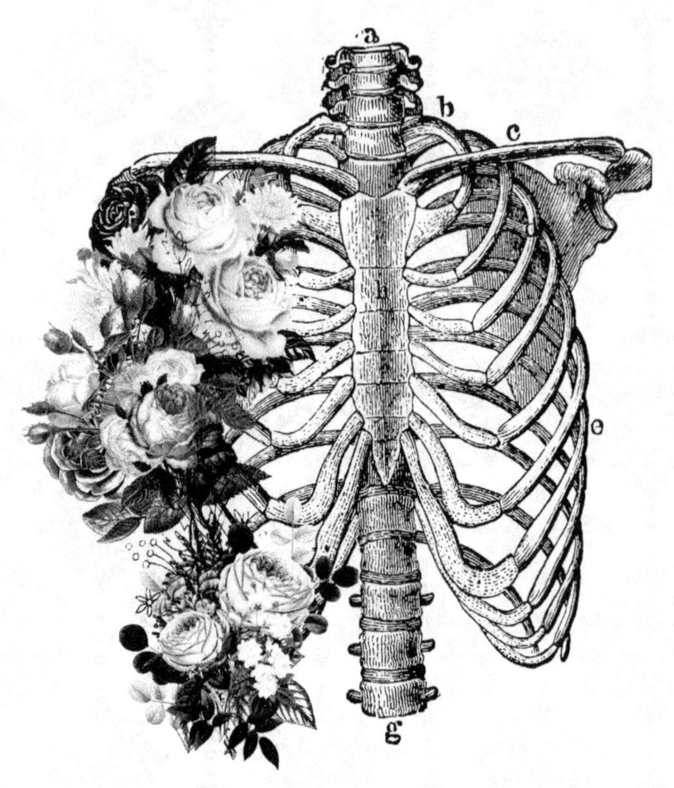
a
b
c
e
g

Bone

Scars

A stitch,
A scar,
A memory.

Untitled

As I tear at the walls of my home, my body
I suffer and I bleed
The loathing bombards the scars freckles and stretch marks.
I try to rebuild; to patch myself up with self-assurances.
Building bricks of love and happiness.
To not grow into any set mold
To blossom into a wildflower:
Fierce, delicate, blooming

Day Break

It must be close to 5 am
I drift between states of consciousness
I drag my index finger along his back
lazily making shapes
feeling the smooth skin
committing this to memory

his breathing even
I'm curious if he knows

I can feel myself slip
sleep overcoming
my finger movements less deliberate
my body shifting to his
for safety, for comfort
needing to have flesh to flesh
as I fall to sleep

Combustion

A dull ember, a trickle that builds with tempted touches.
A hum kisses the air. Distance is the enemy, to our bodies,
the feeling of your heartbeat in my fingertips.

A fire that will consume, maim, fully engulf your entire
essence. Caught with bated breath, a bundle of nerves and
temptations.

A fire so wild only us intertwined will snuff it out with
sweet caress, our noses touch.

Primal

Chapped lips
My entire body thirsty
You deny the basic primal in me
I blink back tears
The wetness burns against the parched hungry cheekbones
Yearning for a simple caress

Rushing the Moment

Fingers running through my hair
Thumb brushes my lower lip
Hand grips my shoulder tightly,
digging in deeply
Blood rushing
Souls seeping into one another
moments bleeding into one
breathing hitched time means nothing

Crawling

Tentacles stretch, curl underneath
Like branches you reach out and intertwine with my roots
Tracing my veins
Dancing up my arm
Swirling and curling toes
As the sensation draws me closer

That First Day

The first day we met, I knew something was there, an electricity or unknowing element hummed within the room that only we felt. I trusted you so easily, fell so fast. I tried to deny it. Even more so when I knew I was in love. I question if it's love because love shouldn't be this hard or hurt like this but at the same time, I know it is because you still haunt my dreams.

Threshold

I am humbled by my pain
I am in awe of it
Could never fathom its evolution
How it ebbs and flows
Pulls me under
Then releases me
Just to drown me yet again
It's an ever-burning flame
Tickling my nerves
Yet can ignite a forest fire
Such an unpredictable enemy

Untitled

From first shared breath
From tangled sheets and limbs intertwined
Giggle, snicker, we shared our secret language
of laughs beneath the covers
Wild abandon; such a sweet escape
We left our troubles at the door

Untitled

Your kiss reminds me I'm alive
Your touch reminds me to breathe
Your words: a sweet song

Battle Scars

I lost the battle
I lost the war
You left my heartless
Crying on the bathroom floor

Bloody Valentine

Crack open my sternum
Rip out my heart
Feel it beat one last time for you

FIREFLY

Luminescence beating down on me
The warmth caressing my cheek
Fingertips brush against my lips
Seducing me with contentment

REVERIE

A fever dream
That cuts to the bone
Falling to pieces
Dripping in sweat
clutching the cold side of the pillow
knotted in sheets
The Passion pulls me through the darkness
Lights my fantasies on fire

PHANTOM

He's always in the back of my mind,
deep in my gut,
and always a part of my heart.
Just thinking about him makes it hard to breathe,
my chest tightens,
and my mind softens for a second.
What is that feeling?
Nostalgia?
Love?
Heartbreak?
I don't know anymore.

Panic Attack

Burning. Snapping.
From my diaphragm,
Trickling up
Scorching and tearing
Tightness- curling inward making it harder to breathe,
Compression like books crushing:
Bearing down on my ribs,
My heartbeat in my ears,
Not gushing, not rushing
A stagnant thump
Reminding me of my suffocation

I TASTE THE AIR

FULL BODIED COFFEE

AND DESPERATION

Foreplay

I could feel his nimble fingers
brushing against my ribs
Making my spine tingle
My hair stands on end
The way he makes me feel when his arms wrap around me
A painful game of cat and mouse

Morphine

I felt myself slipping away when a faint voice broke through. A woman with kind eyes and latex gloves sat next to me; the process of quick relief had begun.

 I held my body still as I felt the medication slithering from the tube into my awaiting vein. In a second my entire body tensed, the feeling of fire coursing through my blood vessels. I knew the instant the pharmaceutical hit my brain.

I felt as if I was sinking down to the bottom of a swimming pool, when the sun glints on the surface of the water and slightly blinds. I felt so heavy then.

Surrounded in a cocoon of numbness that seemed to be suffocating me as each second passed. I could not breathe. I still felt every pulsating beat of time.

I could feel the blood stammering into my head and every vein. The air cracked with anticipation like before a lightning strike, thick and humming.

 My lungs began to burn as I quickly realized it had been too long since my last breath. A gray fog danced on the outside of my vision but something inside me could not inhale.

 I gasped as instinct took over. I inhaled a crisp breath and felt a delicious numbing sensation encompass my body, melting my pain away like ice cream on a summer's day. I was warm, fuzzy, and content.

Withered

If my withered body
could speak of all the stifled words,
Tell of the aches and the pains,
The pleasures and the comforts,
Would you bother to listen?

Untitled

Your love defines me
It's in my bones
Twitching in my muscles
The spark in my nerve fibers
The blood in my veins
Every ounce of me breathes for you

The Writer's Disease

My medication has clouded my mind from the words
I so desperately seek.
They seem so out of reach
It physically hurts
I feel empty and too full at the same time.
Too much emotion pent up and brimming,
trying to get out
but when I try to write every word recoils in fear.
I only feel like myself when I'm writing
when I find the right words
lining up and stringing them together.
The final piece a beautiful pearl necklace
or complicated spider's web.
Both are so elegant in their own way.
I wish I could get my mind back on the words,
just 26 letters,
yet they elude me, and I feel incomplete.
My DNA is lacking.

Can't Sleep

Insomnia subdues my senses,
Invades them until sleep seems like a far-off dream.

The Animal Within

I feel feral.
Dizzy and anxious.
I can't catch my breath.
My stomach churns.
Tears burn down my freckled face.
They don't release the agony
or cease my mind from racing.
Like a caged lion,
There is no freedom.

Combat

My body is my enemy
It is my sanctuary
I fight the agony constant in my bones
Adoring the ever-beating heart
 Every breath is a reminder
that I am at war
That I exist in two realities
Pain and Pleasure

Hush

Like a thick fog
You came into my life
Slowly then surrounding me all at once
Eerie yet beautiful
Suffocating in the silence
Swirling; pulling me into oblivion

UNTITLED

I can smell the whiskey on his breath
His weight shifting
Hands roaming
Bites my lip
Speech is slurred
Time is blurred
and I'm stone-cold sober.

Invaded

I felt as if I was being filleted rib to rib. Searing skin as his hand moved over my body. His eyes swimming with greed and wantonness, a desire to tear me limb from limb.

My body ached to run but exhausted from fighting a mental battle for hours before. He had won both my mind and my body too quickly. His smile too sharp and filled with malice.

 I should have caught it but I had been too naive, drunk, and thrown to the snake by my friends. He moved with intention, to insight fear and pain with every inch.

The sweat dripped from my naked body as I twisted, trying to loosen the grip he had on me; but that only drove him on. His breath swarmed my senses, ripe with cheap whiskey.

 My body betrayed me as it responded to his touch, I felt as sick with myself as I was with him. How could MY body like this feeling as he slithered and danced into the crevices of my broken body?

My mind tried to fight the feelings washing over me as he played me like a violin, sliding over each note with great ease and no feeling. I pushed everything from my consciousness, trying to clear the plight from my mind.

His nakedness was a sign of rebellion. A captain of his ship in which he navigated with precise gestures. Everyone made to make me weaker, to submit to him.

His hands-on my wrists only tightened as I grappled with the vise grip, he had on them. He laughed then, maniacal, sadistic, and not at all human. The sound reverberated off the walls of the studio apartment and scraped at my eardrums.

Every memory of self-defense class ran through my brain, but my body would not comply with any orders because of the sheer exhaustion it had been subjected to. Muscles tight, stretched to their limit, joints twisted and pulled in uncomfortable positions.

Every inch of movement brought more pain. He stood slightly above me on the bed, his eyes dancing with cruelty as he explained what he was going to do next. My body ached with tension, but I bit my lip and kicked up as he moved forward.

My knee slammed into his nether regions and he fell next to me in pain. I took my chance and stood up quickly. I felt dizzy, the haze danced around the outer corners of my eyes as I looked for my clothes and quickly threw them on haphazardly.

He scrambled to regain control, but I already had my hand on the door and was determined to escape. I shot him a glance that could kill a pack of wolves and slipped out the door, stumbling all the way to my car.

I could hear him shouting but I pushed my weakened body to its breaking point to get inside the safe haven of the four-door SUV. I locked the doors and let my body relax, every fiber on fire from the torture it had just endured.

I let a single tear fall before I pushed my emotions down, locking them away. I turned on the ignition and peeled out of the driveway trying to get as much asphalt between me and this haunted complex.

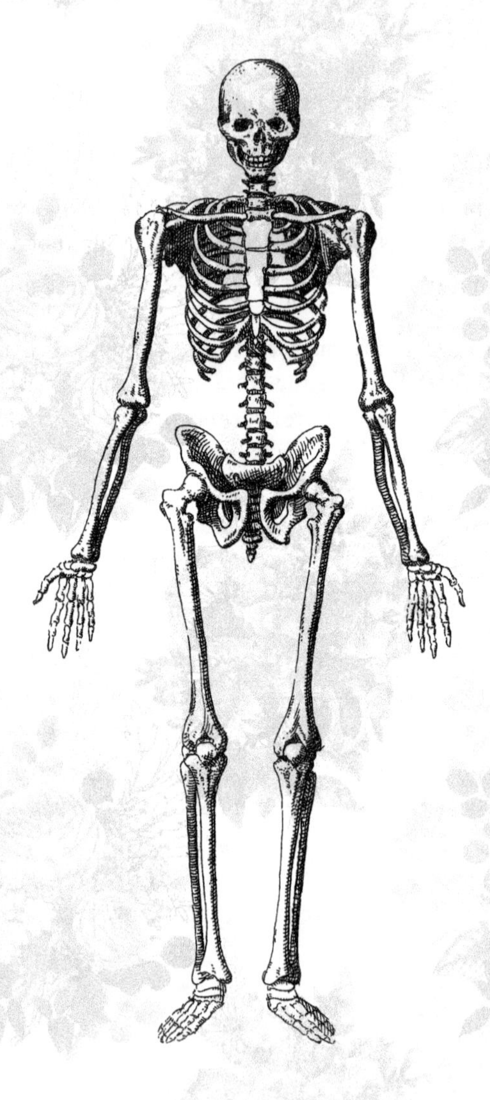

Thank you for reading, for giving my words life. Thank you for spending your time with my thoughts. This book was a journey dissecting myself and my emotions while going through some of the most difficult times in my life and giving them a life of their own.

- Kelly

MY THOUGHTS AND LIFE
@WritesTheUnsaid on Instagram

Acknowledgements

I want to thank Matt Allen for listening to me prattle on about words and definitions and synonyms; for letting me talk poetry when he feels like he doesn't know anything about it. He is my inspiration. He is also the only one who could ground me when I felt like the words left me. He keeps me sane.

Thank you mom, Diane, for encouraging my writing and for listening to different versions of the same poem and for always offering constructive criticism. You made me a better poet.

I want to thank Rachel Clift for taking my manuscript and breathing life into it. For taking my words and making the book into what you see today. She took my inspiration for the cover and made exactly what I wanted. She brought it to life. Thank you again for everything you did to make my dream a reality.

About the Author

Kelly Curry is an old soul based in Lake Tahoe, California where she lives with a menagerie of animals. When Kelly is not writing, she is collecting books she plans to read. Breath and Bone is her debut poetry book.

DEATH COMES TO COLLECT BEAUTY

Johann Theodor de Bry, 1596